Seashells by the Seashore

By Marianne Berkes
Illustrated by Robert Noreika

Dawn Publications

Sue walks along the seashore
warmed by the sun.
Picking up seashells one by one.

Here's a pretty Periwinkle.
What a work of art!

Let's find some more shells;
We're off to a good start.

Periwinkle

Kitten's
Paw

Seashells tumble
From the ocean blue.

Find a tiny Kitten's Paw
So Sue can have two.

Periwinkle

Kitten's
Paw

Jingle
Shell

Once creatures lived
In these shells from the sea.

Here's a fragile Jingle Shell.
Now there are three.

Periwinkle

Kitten's
Paw

Jingle
Shell

Olive Shell

When the animals die,
The shells wash up to shore.

A smooth and empty Olive Shell
Will bring us up to four.

Periwinkle

Kitten's
Paw

Jingle
Shell

Olive Shell

Scallop
Shell

We're getting good at "shelling."
No time to swim or dive.

A Scallop has a fan shape—
That makes five!

Periwinkle

Kitten's
Paw

Jingle
Shell

Olive Shell

Scallop
Shell

Whelk
Shell

So many seashells
That we can mix.

If we find a Whelk Shell
There will be six.

Periwinkle

Kitten's Paw

Jingle Shell

Olive Shell

Scallop Shell

Whelk Shell

Oyster Shell

How the seashells glisten
In the sun that shines from heaven.

Here's a bumpy Oyster Shell
So that makes seven.

Periwinkle

Kitten's Paw

Jingle Shell

Olive Shell

Scallop Shell

Whelk Shell

Oyster Shell

Slipper Shell

The tide is rolling in
And it's getting pretty late.

This shell looks like a slipper!
Now we have eight.

Periwinkle

Kitten's Paw

Jingle Shell

Olive Shell

Scallop Shell

Whelk Shell

Oyster Shell

Slipper Shell

Moon Shell

We're scouring through the beach sand.
Lots of shells are fine.

We want to find a Moon Shell
To bring us up to nine!

Periwinkle

Kitten's Paw

Jingle Shell

Olive Shell

Scallop Shell

Whelk Shell

Oyster Shell

Slipper Shell

Moon Shell

Pen Shell

"I've got some really awesome shells"
Sue tells her brother, Ben.

He's found a spiny pen shell.
Now there are ten.

"Do you think she'll like them?"
Ben asks Sue.

"Grandma walked this beach, Ben,
Just like me and you.

"She loved to look for different shells
Of every shape and size.

"And so these treasures that we've found
Will be a great surprise."

Periwinkle

Kitten's Paw

Jingle Shell

Olive Shell

Scallop Shell

Whelk Shell

Oyster Shell

Slipper Shell

Moon Shell

Pen Shell

Ark Shell

"I've got one too!"
Says Ben's friend, Evan.

He adds a heavy Ark Shell
And that makes eleven.

Periwinkle

Kitten's Paw

Jingle Shell

Olive Shell

Scallop Shell

Whelk Shell

Oyster Shell

Slipper Shell

Moon Shell

Pen Shell

Ark Shell

Cockle Shell

They'll scrub the seashell sculptures
To put on Grandma's shelves.

Let's find a Cockle Shell
So there will be twelve.

Periwinkle

Kitten's
Paw

Jingle
Shell

Olive Shell

Scallop
Shell

Whelk
Shell

Oyster
Shell

Slipper
Shell

Moon
Shell

Pen Shell

Ark
Shell

Cockle
Shell

Twelve seashell treasures
Are in Sue's pail.

But wait! What's this?
A slimy sea snail?

That's the mollusk inside,
Alive as it can be.

We need to take him down
To his home in the sea.

Evan takes the Whelk Shell
Down to the shore.

The creature living deep inside
Will crawl around once more.

"Happy Birthday, Grandma!
And many, many more.

We have a special gift for you—
Seashells from the seashore."

Shell sculptures are some of the most incredible designs in nature. There are many kinds. In this story some are large and some are small. Others are long or round, and some are bumpy or smooth. Some are even named for what they look like.

Seashells are made by the animals that live inside them. These sea creatures are called mollusks. A mollusk has a soft body that needs protection from a hard shell.

Most of the shells found on the beach can be put into two groups. One group is called "univalves." "Uni" means "one," so they have only one shell. Univalves are mollusks that move on one foot. Periwinkles, olive shells and whelks are part of this group.

The second group is called "bivalves." "Bi" means two. The mollusk lives between the two parts of this double shell, which is joined by a hinge. When the shell is open, it can eat by taking food from the water. When danger threatens, the two shells quickly snap shut. Oysters, scallops and ark shells are part of this group.

Turn the page for a description of the shells that are in this book. Can you name the univalves and the bivalves? Which ones are smooth or bumpy? Which ones are named for what they look like? Next time you go to the beach, look for these shells, or other favorites, to put in your bucket. Collect only empty shells; never remove live mollusks from their homes. It is a good idea to scrub the shells in warm, soapy water. Once they have been cleaned, they can be beautifully displayed.

Periwinkles have a distinctive shape. Most of them come to a point and have banded lines around them. This univalve lives in marshes and on rocks, and can live out of water longer than other sea creatures. The empty shells found on beaches can be smooth or prickly.

Kitten Paws are small bivalves whose shells look like a paw. After a long time in the sun, they fade to a lustrous white. Usually half of the shell washes up on the beach, while the other half remains attached to rocks or other shells with a powerful glue the mollusk makes.

Jingle Shells are thin bivalves that you can see through. The top shell, which is cupped and pearly, washes ashore more often than the lower shell. There is a hole in the lower shell where the animal anchors itself. People string these shells together to make wind chimes that tinkle.

Olive Shells are smooth and glossy because the mollusk wraps its soft body, commonly called its foot, around the shell and keeps it polished. It is a univalve that is long and shaped like a tube. Some olive shells have greenish gray with reddish brown zigzag markings. These are called 'lettered' shells. They are usually found buried in the sand.

Scallop Shells usually have unequal bivalves. The lower one is raised while the upper one is flat with beautiful colors. The calico scallop, which has equal bivalves, can be a mixture of white, rose, purple, brown and yellow-orange with many ribs running from the hinge to the outer edge.

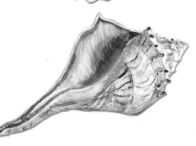

Whelk Shells are moderately large univalves that can be found alive in shallow waters and mud flats. They have a solid shell that narrows to a long pointy open canal. The shell sculpture is somewhat varied. A whelk is a sea snail that stretches out a big foot that it crawls around on.

Oyster Shells are unequal bivalves that are large and heavy. They are easy to identify because they resemble elongated feet. The rough and bumpy shells are usually long and somewhat curved, and vary in shape depending on how and where they lived. Many people use this mollusk as a source for food.

Slipper Shells are found among rocks and on other shells in shallow water. You might also see them attached to each other in a pile. A thin shelf covers half of the shell like the top of a slipper. That is how this cup-shaped, light-colored univalve with tan spots got its name.

Moon Shells are snails that feed on other univalves. They are found burrowed in the sand at low tide. Shiny and smooth, their violet and brown color tends to fade when the shells wash ashore. On top of the shell there is a beautiful swirl with an eye in the middle.

Pen Shells are large delicate brown bivalves. They have at least 15 rows of tubular spines that look like a fan. Other sea creatures sometimes attach themselves to the dead shells so when you first see them on the beach, they may look ugly. But the inside looks like mother-of-pearl.

Ark Shells are a type of clam. These bivalves are heavy and have many ribs. These strong shells sometimes attach themselves to the undersides of rocks. One kind of ark shell, the cut-ribbed ark, is long and has a dark mossy coating. But after it has tumbled around in the surf, it is often pure white when it washes up on the beach.

Cockle Shells are bivalves that vary in size from 1/2 inch to 5 inches. They look like a heart when they are closed—nature's own valentine. The inside usually is a beautiful purple or pink. These shells are often used for ashtrays and small containers.

Formerly an early childhood educator and children's theater director in New York, Marianne Berkes now lives in Florida where she is a children's librarian. "Miss Marianne," as the children at the Palm Beach County Library know her, enjoys telling stories about animals and nature. She also visits local schools where she presents special storytelling programs about the books she has written. **Seashells by the Seashore** *is her third book. Living near the ocean, Marianne enjoys swimming, boating and walking the beach, where she often picks up beautiful shells to add to her collection. She dedicates this book to her husband, Roger, her shipmate on the sea of life.*

Robert Noreika is a watercolorist with a passion for nature and art. He attended the Paier College of Art in Hamden, Connecticut and has his studio in an Arts Center in Avon, Connecticut. He has always loved to comb the beaches and hike in woods, and now he does so with his wife, Chris, and seven year-old daughter, Sarah. This is the fourth book he has illustrated.

A FEW OTHER SELECTIONS FROM THE DAWN PUBLICATIONS BOOKSHELF

Over in the Ocean: In a Coral Reef by Marianne Berkes. This coral reef is a marine nursery, teeming with mamas and babies! In the age-old way of kids and fish, children will count and clap to the rhythm of "Over in the Meadow" while puffer fish "puff," gruntfish "grunt" and seahorses "flutter."

Over in the Jungle: A Rainforest Rhyme by Marianne Berkes, a companion to *Over in the Ocean*, features a tropical rainforest teeming with monkeys that hoot, ocelots that pounce, and boas that squeeze! Eye-popping illustrations by Jeanette Canyon are all in polymer clay.

This is the Sea that Feeds Us by Robert F. Baldwin. In simple cumulative verse, this book explores the oceans' fabulous food web that reaches all the way from plankton to people.

Salmon Stream by Carol Reed-Jones, follows the life cycle of salmon, who hatch in a stream, travel the world, and return to their birthplace against staggering odds.

Eliza and the Dragonfly by Susie Rinehart. This charming story revolves around the beauty and wonder of the hidden world that can be found in a local pond.

Forest Bright, Forest Night by Jennifer Ward. Take a peek into the forest in the daytime, then flip the book to see the same forest at nighttime. Count the animals, and see who is asleep and who is busy!

All Around Me, I See by Laya Steinberg. With eyes wide open to the wonders of nature, a child, tired from her hike, sleeps—and in her dream, flies like a bird and marvels at the life around her.

Stickeen: John Muir and the Brave Little Dog by John Muir as retold by Donnell Rubay. In this classic true story, the relationship between the great naturalist and a small dog is changed forever by their adventure on a glacier in Alaska.

A Drop Around the World by Barbara Shaw McKinney, follows a single drop of water—from snow to steam, from polluted to purified, from stratus cloud to subterranean crack. Drop inspires respect for water's unique role on Earth. (Teacher's Guide available.)

A Swim through the Sea by Kristin Joy Pratt, is a best-selling favorite by this young "Eco-star" author-illustrator. Her other books are *A Walk in the Rainforest, A Fly in the Sky,* and most recently *Salamander Rain: A Lake and Pond Journal* and *Saguaro Moon: A Desert Journal.*

Dawn Publications is dedicated to inspiring in children a deeper understanding and appreciation for all life on Earth. To view our full list of titles or to order, please visit our web site at www.dawnpub.com, or call 800-545-7475.

Library of Congress Cataloging-in-Publication Data

Berkes, Marianne Collins.
   Seashells by the seashore / by Marianne Berkes ; illustrated by
Robert Noreika.
      p. cm. — (A sharing nature with children book)
   Summary: A child and her companions collect a variety of seashells
from one to twelve.
   ISBN 1-58469-034-8 (pbk.) — ISBN 1-58469-035-6 (hardback)
   1. Shells—Juvenile literature. [1. Shells. 2. Counting.]   I.
Noreika, Robert, ill. II. Title. III. Series.
   QL405.2 .B47 2002
   594.147'7—dc21
                                        2001005459

Dawn Publications
12402 Bitney Springs Road
Nevada City, CA 95959
530-274-7775
nature@dawnpub.com

Printed in China, May 2009

10 9 8 7 6
First Edition
Design and computer production by Andrea Miles